Col

C000003235

by Ian Ansdell

Lang**Syne**

PUBLISHING

WRITING *to* REMEMBER

LangSyne
PUBLISHING
WRITING *to* REMEMBER

79 Main Street, Newtongrange,
Midlothian EH22 4NA
Tel: 0131 344 0414   Fax: 0845 075 6085
E-mail: info@lang-syne.co.uk
www.langsyneshop.co.uk

Design by Dorothy Meikle
Printed by Printwell Ltd
© Lang Syne Publishers Ltd 2020

978-1-85217-212-1

Colquhoun

SEPT NAMES INCLUDE:

Calhoun
Cahoon
Cohoon
Cowan
Cowen
Culchone
Ingram
Kilpatrick
King
Kirkpatrick
Laing
MacAchounich
MacCowan
MacClintock
MacLintock
MacMains
MacManus
MacOwan

Colquhoun

MOTTO:
Si je puis
(If I can).

CREST:
A hart's head couped Gules,
attired Argent.

TERRITORY:
Luss, Loch Lomond.

Chapter one:

The origins of the clan system

by Rennie McOwan

The original Scottish clans of the Highlands and the great families of the Lowlands and Borders were gatherings of families, relatives, allies and neighbours for mutual protection against rivals or invaders.

Scotland experienced invasion from the Vikings, the Romans and English armies from the south. The Norman invasion of what is now England also had an influence on land-holding in Scotland. Some of these invaders stayed on and in time became 'Scottish'.

The word clan derives from the Gaelic language term 'clann', meaning children, and it was first used many centuries ago as communities were formed around tribal lands in glens and mountain fastnesses.

The format of clans changed over the centuries, but at its best the chief and his family held the land on behalf of all, like trustees, and the ordinary clansmen and women believed they had a blood relationship with the founder of their clan.

There were two way duties and obligations. An inadequate chief could be deposed and replaced by someone of greater ability.

Clan people had an immense pride in race. Their relationship with the chief was like adult children to a father and they had a real dignity.

The concept of clanship is very old and a more feudal notion of authority gradually crept in.

Pictland, for instance, was divided into seven principalities ruled by feudal leaders who were the strongest and most charismatic leaders of their particular groups.

By the sixth century the 'British' kingdoms of Strathclyde, Lothian and Celtic Dalriada (Argyll) had emerged and Scotland, as one nation, began to take shape in the time of King Kenneth MacAlpin.

Some chiefs claimed descent from

ancient kings which may not have been accurate in every case.

By the twelfth and thirteenth centuries the clans and families were more strongly brought under the central control of Scottish monarchs.

Lands were awarded and administered more and more under royal favour, yet the power of the area clan chiefs was still very great.

The long wars to ensure Scotland's independence against the expansionist ideas of English monarchs extended the influence of some clans and reduced the lands of others.

Those who supported Scotland's greatest king, Robert the Bruce, were awarded the territories of the families who had opposed his claim to the Scottish throne.

In the Scottish Borders country – the notorious Debatable Lands – the great families built up a ferocious reputation for providing warlike men accustomed to raiding into England and occasionally fighting one another.

Chiefs had the power to dispense justice and to confiscate lands and clan warfare produced a society where martial virtues – courage, hardiness, tenacity – were greatly admired.

Gradually the relationship between the clans and the Crown became strained as Scottish monarchs became more orientated to life in the Lowlands and, on occasion, towards England.

The Highland clans spoke a different language, Gaelic, whereas the language of Lowland Scotland and the court was Scots and in more modern times, English.

Highlanders dressed differently, had different customs, and their wild mountain land sometimes seemed almost foreign to people living in the Lowlands.

It must be emphasised that Gaelic culture was very rich and story-telling, poetry, piping, the clarsach (harp) and other music all flourished and were greatly respected.

Highland culture was different from other parts of Scotland but it was not inferior or less sophisticated.

Central Government, whether in London or Edinburgh, sometimes saw the Gaelic clans as

*"The spirit of the clan means much to
thousands of people"*

a challenge to their authority and some sent expeditions into the Highlands and west to crush the power of the Lords of the Isles.

Nevertheless, when the eighteenth century Jacobite Risings came along the cause of the Stuarts was mainly supported by Highland clans.

The word Jacobite comes from the Latin for James – Jacobus. The Jacobites wanted to restore the exiled Stuarts to the throne of Britain.

The monarchies of Scotland and England became one in 1603 when King James VI of Scotland (1st of England) gained the English throne after Queen Elizabeth died.

The Union of Parliaments of Scotland and England, the Treaty of Union, took place in 1707.

Some Highland clans, of course, and Lowland families opposed the Jacobites and supported the incoming Hanoverians.

After the Jacobite cause finally went down at Culloden in 1746 a kind of ethnic cleansing took place. The power of the chiefs was curtailed. Tartan and the pipes were banned in law.

Many emigrated, some because they

wanted to, some because they were evicted by force. In addition, many Highlanders left for the cities of the south to seek work.

Many of the clan lands became home to sheep and deer shooting estates.

But the warlike traditions of the clans and the great Lowland and Border families lived on, with their descendants fighting bravely for freedom in two world wars.

Remember the men from whence you came, says the Gaelic proverb, and to that could be added the role of many heroic women.

The spirit of the clan, of having roots, whether Highland or Lowland, means much to thousands of people.

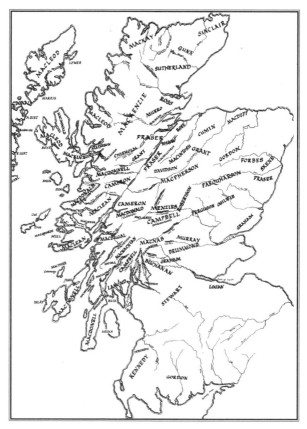

A map of the clans' homelands

Chapter two:

Sons of the fair maid

The Colquhoun family came into being when Umfridus (Humphrey) de Kilpatrick was given the lands and barony of Colquhoun in Dunbartonshire by the Earl of Lennox around 1241. Humphrey took the place-name as his own name, and the clan was born.

His grandson, Ingelram, lived in the reign of Alexander III and Ingleram's son, Humphrey de Colquhoun, witnessed a charter of Malcolm, fifth Earl of Lennox, between the years 1292-1333.

It was Humphrey's own son, Sir Robert de Colquhoun, who truly brought the dynasty into being when in 1368 he married the Fair Maid of Luss – the daughter and heiress of Godfry, Lord of Luss, on the banks of Loch Lomond.

Sir Robert was in due course named

Lord of Colquhoun and Luss in a charter dated 1368, and ever since then the family has borne the title Colquhoun of Colquhoun and Luss.

A grand title – but perhaps with a humble meaning. William Tytler, the eighteenth century historian and antiquarian, described Colquhoun as "an obscure word, which occurs nowhere else – conjectured by a learned friend to be 'keepers of the dogs', from the Gaelic root Gillen-au-con – abbreviated, Gillecon, Culquhoun."

Chapter three:

Bandit country

As essentially lowland landowners on the fringe of the Highlands, the Colquhouns had to contend with wild neighbours to the north and west.

Sir John Colquhoun was appointed governor of Dumbarton Castle by King James I, and soon made it his business to make life difficult for raiders from the Highlands and Islands who descended on the Dunbartonshire lowlands to plunder and destroy.

They in turn plotted revenge against him. Successfully, as it turned out. In 1439, Sir John was invited to parley with their chiefs on the Loch Lomond island of Inchmurrin.

Naively accepting their overtures in good faith, he went to meet them with only a few companions instead of the large armed company which the occasion might have been thought to require.

He paid the price, being immediately attacked and murdered by a gang led by two notorious robber chiefs, Murdoch Gibson and Lachlan Maclean of Duart.

It was not the first such encounter between 'Heilanman' and Lowlander – nor would it be the last or most notorious.

In 1592, a raiding party of Macgregors and Macfarlanes was chased back over the Highland Line by Sir Humphrey Colquhoun, leading a force of clansmen and neighbouring lairds.

Coming off second best in the ensuing battle, the Lowlanders retreated to the Colquhoun castle of Bannachra where they were beseiged by the lawless reivers.

Sir Humphrey should have been safe in his stronghold – but treachery would be the undoing of a Colquhoun once more.

One of his servants – himself a Colquhoun – shone a light on his master as he led him past a loophole on the winding stair leading to his room. A single arrow fired from the darkness outside went straight through Humphrey's heart.

Another version of the tale shows all participants in the incident in an even worse light. It is said that Sir Humphrey was beseiged by Macfarlanes because of a love affair with the wife of their chief, and that the fatal arrow was shot by his brother, Iain, who hoped to speed up his succession as head of the family.

In the event, Iain was executed in Edinburgh for the crime. One chronicler recounts that the amorous Sir Humphrey's body was mutilated "in a peculiarly revolting though appropriate manner", and served up as a dish for his lover, Lady Macfarlane.

Moreover: "So little regard did these savage freebooters pay to the laws of chivalry that they brutally violated the person of Jean Colquhoun, the fair and helpless daughter of Sir Humphrey."

Chapter four:

Macgregor no more

Whatever the truth of Sir Humphrey's demise, he was succeeded by another younger brother, Alexander, under whom the most far-reaching clashes between Highlander and Lowlander took place.

In December, 1602, the Macgregors mounted a raid on the laird of Luss's lands in Glenfinlas, rustling sheep and cattle, and slaughtering many of his tenants.

It was the last straw for a clan which had complained many times to the Privy Council about the Macgregors' conduct without receiving redress.

This time, Alexander went directly to the court of King James IV at Stirling accompanied by sixty or so wailing Colquhoun women carrying the bloodied shirts of their dead and wounded menfolk.

No matter the rumour that it was sheep's

blood which stained some of the garments – the appalled monarch commissioned Colquhoun to bring down the weight of law on the Macgregors.

That lawless family was not inclined to wait for matters to resolve themselves, and Allaster Macgregor of Glenstrae led a band of 400 of his own clansmen as well as Camerons, armed to the teeth, into the lands of Luss.

Alexander, meantime, had assembled as many as 300 horsemen and 500 warriors on foot. The two forces came together in Glenfruin on February 7, 1603, with disastrous consequences for both sides.

Colquhoun's superior numbers were cancelled out by Macgregor's superior tactics. The Highlander split his strength in two and trapped Alexander in the glen. With Macgregors in front and behind, and no means of escape, the Colquhouns suffered a terrible defeat.

Alexander himself only just escaped with his life after his horse had been killed

under him, but 140 of his clansmen were slaughtered and many more wounded, including women and children.

The Macgregors rounded off their victory by wreaking havoc on Colquhoun land, burning houses and steadings and stealing hundreds of horses, cattle, sheep and goats.

It was a tremendous coup, but the timing could not have been worse. James VI of Scotland was on the point of leaving for London to become James I of England. Engaged in the epoch-making Union of the Crowns of two ancient enemies, the last thing he needed was the distraction of lawlessness in his own back yard.

Alaster Macgregor and another thirty-four participants in the massacre were executed, and everyone else who had participated on the Highlanders' side was banned under penalty of death from carrying any weapon – except a pointless knife to eat their meat.

But the wider judgement of the Privy Council, delivered just two days before James quit Scotland in April 1603, could not have been more severe. The names of Gregor and Macgregor was abolished forever. Clan members had to change their names or face death, and the capital penalty also awaited anyone who gave food or shelter to any of them.

The bandits had become outlaws. And while the Macgregor name would ironically live on in fame and fable through the exploits of Rob Roy, the Colquhouns were at last able to settle down to lives of civilised prosperity.

The feud had its postscript in the early 1800s when Sir John Murray Macgregor, at the invitation of Sir James Colquhoun, visited Glenfruin and shook hands on the battlefield. This touching reconciliation was later sealed when Sir John, then in his eighties, danced a Highland reel with Sir James' daughter, Catherine, on the summit of Ben Lomond.

Chapter five:

The devil take him

The centuries since Glenfruin have been relatively quiet for the Colquhouns compared with the turbulent history of other clans, but not entirely without incident.

Alexander's son, Sir John Colquhoun, married Lilias Graham, eldest sister of the great Marquis of Montrose, before running off with her younger sister, Lady Catherine Graham.

A sufficient breach of social etiquette, one might think – but in the spirit of the times Sir John was accused of having used sorcery to entice Catherine. Pursued by tales of witchcraft, love potions and enchanted jewels, he fled to Italy and died there, outlawed and excommunicated.

The family kept its head down during the Jacobite risings, and typical of this clan of douce improvers was Sir James Colquhoun, who in the late 1700s founded the town of Helensburgh, naming it after his wife, Lady Helen, a sister of the 17th Earl of Sutherland.

During the First World War, Sir Iain Colquhoun was lightweight boxing champion of the British Army, kept a pet lion in the trenches, killed a Prussian officer with his revolver and five Bavarians with an improvised club, and won the Distinguished Service Order.

Chapter six:

Lovely Luss

Two place-names are inseparable from the history of Clan Colquhoun – those of Rossdhu and Luss itself.

Named after the Gaelic 'ros dubh' for the 'black headland', the ancient lands of Rossdhu became the site of a castle built in the fifteenth century by Sir John Colquhoun, Great Chamberlain of Scotland and joint Ambassador to England.

Now they are home to a magnificent Georgian mansion house, with the ruins of the castle behind and the banks of Loch Lomond in front. Mainly built by Sir James Colquhoun of Luss in 1774, its portico and wings were added by his successor.

Open to the public for a time last century, Rossdhu lay unused for many years with its fine interior suffering vandalism or theft before being restored to much of its former glory as the club house for Loch Lomond Golf Course.

As to the village of Luss, James Denholm said of it in 1804: "The houses, in general, appear exceedingly uncomfortable. They are mostly built of loose stones, perhaps with a layer of turf betwixt each row are covered with rushes; the produce of the Loch. They are likewise very low and the door, before which is a thick layer of fern, so difficult to access that a person must stoop considerably before he can enter.

"The interior in general corresponds to their outward appearance, being dark and often full of smoke which is discharged as plentiful out of the window and the door as the ordinary aperture."

Such conditions might have been satisfactory for centuries, but the times were changing. Visiting Loch Lomondside in 1838 for the first time in twelve years, the High Court judge Lord Cockburn wrote in his diary: "I am more and more struck with its magnificence and loveliness. The church of Luss is, from its charming position, beautiful as ever."

However, he added: "But the dirt and squalid wretchedness of the houses and people of that village is a disgrace to the landlords. Such abomination, in such a scene, is one of the unanswerable scandals of Scotland.

"The lairds who permit it are the chief brutes. And how little it would take to charm the poor people into a higher state of existence, and to make their promontory a paradise. At present, God has planted a garden there, and man a hog-stye."

The 'brutes' took the point eventually. The Imperial Gazetteer of Scotland noted of Luss in 1868: "About two years ago, Sir James Colquhoun made known a resolution to sweep away its rude straggling huts, and to rebuild it on a regular, specific plan.

"Its own character, therefore, will be put into keeping with the beauty of its site. It has a good inn, and is much frequented by tasteful tourists."

And tasteful tourists continue to relish Luss, now a conservation village famous as the home of the long-running – but now defunct – TV saga *High Road*.

Sir James also had the present church built in 1875 as a memorial to his father who died along with five ghillies in a drowning accident off Inchtavannach.

It boasts a magnificent roof of Scots pine, a stained glass window dedicated to Clan Colquhoun and an effigy of the medieval bishop Robert Colquhoun of Argyll. On the north wall is the Macfarlane Stone, dating from 1612, which carries the inscription: 'After deathe remains virtue'.

The Clan Colquhoun Museum and Visitor Centre opened in Luss in 2001 and is open to the public from May until October each year.

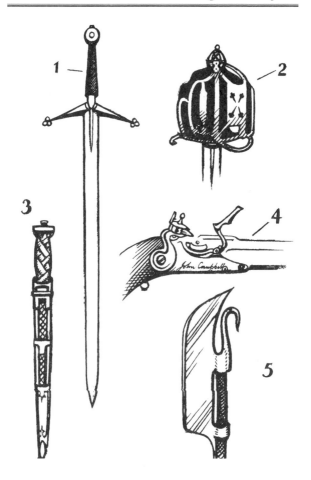

Highland weapons

1)   The claymore or two-handed sword
     (fifteenth or early sixteenth century)

2)   Basket hilt of broadsword
     made in Stirling, 1716

3)   Highland dirk
     (eighteenth century)

4)   Steel pistol *(detail)* made in Doune

5)   Head of Lochaber Axe as carried
     in the '45 and earlier